Jul 2020

STARS OF SPORTS

GIANNIS ANTETOKOUNMPO

BASKETBALL POWERHOUSE

■ ■ by Matt Chandler

CAPSTONE PRESS
a capstone imprint

Stars of Sports is published by Capstone Press, an imprint of Capstone.
1710 Roe Crest Drive, North Mankato, Minnesota 56003
www.capstonepub.com

Library of Congress Cataloging-in-Publication Data
Names: Chandler, Matt, author.
Title: Giannis Antetokounmpo : basketball powerhouse / Matt Chandler.
Description: North Mankato : Capstone Press, [2020] | Includes
    bibliographical references and index. | Audience: Ages 8-11 | Audience:
    Grades 4-6 | Summary: "As the youngest player in the National Basketball
    Association during his rookie season, Giannis Antetokounmpo looked like
    a rising star. At almost seven feet tall, he would become an All-Star
    Game starter and winner of the NBA's most improved player award. Giannis
    went from selling toys and sunglasses to help his family get by to
    playing in the NBA and turning heads with his power and grace. Get all
    the facts on Giannis's extraordinary rise in basketball in this exciting
    biography"-- Provided by publisher.
Identifiers: LCCN 2019039779 (print) | LCCN 2019039780 (ebook) | ISBN
    9781543591712 (hardcover) | ISBN 9781543591859 (pdf)
Subjects: LCSH: Antetokounmpo, Giannis, 1994--Juvenile literature. |
    Basketball players--United States--Biography--Juvenile literature.
Classification: LCC GV884.A56 C43 2020 (print) | LCC GV884.A56 (ebook) |
    DDC 796.323092 [B]--dc23
LC record available at https://lccn.loc.gov/2019039779
LC ebook record available at https://lccn.loc.gov/2019039780

Editorial Credits
Editor: Hank Musolf; Designer: Ashlee Suker; Media Researcher: Eric Gohl;
Production Specialist: Laura Manthe

Image Credits
Associated Press: 9, Mary Altaffer, 5; Newscom: Reuters/Athit Perawongmetha, 27,
Reuters/Keith Bedford, 11, TNS/Jeff Siner, 28, UPI/Jim Ruymen, 13, USA Today
Sports/Benny Sieu, cover, USA Today Sports/Bob Donnan, 19, USA Today Sports/
Jeff Hanisch, 21, 23, 24, USA Today Sports/Jerry Lai, 15, 17, USA Today Sports/John
E. Sokolowski, 22, ZUMA Press/Wassilios Aswestopoulos, 6; Shutterstock: EFKS, 1

All internet sites appearing in back matter were available and accurate when this
book was sent to press.

Direct Quotations
Page 12, from March 27, 2018. CBS article "Giannis Antetokounmpo, the Milwaukee
Bucks' 'Greek Freak'", https://www.cbsnews.com
Page 28, from May 26, 2019. NBA.com article "'A lot of room to grow' -- Bucks,
Giannis eager to learn from disappointing finish to breakthrough season", https://
www.nba.com

Printed in the United States of America.
PA99

TABLE OF CONTENTS

Glossary terms are **BOLD** on first use.

"THE GREEK FREAK"

Milwaukee Bucks forward Giannis Antetokounmpo is nicknamed the "Greek Freak." How did he get that nickname? By doing what seemed impossible on the court. On February 6, 2018, the Bucks took on the New York Knicks. Antetokounmpo, who is 6 feet, 11 inches (210 centimeters) tall, showed off his unique talents in one great play.

The Bucks were ahead by 12 points. It was the third quarter. Bucks guard Chris Middleton stole a pass. He broke toward the basket. Only one Knicks player, Tim Hardaway Jr., was back to defend. Close to the hoop, Middleton passed the ball to Antetokounmpo. Hardaway was in the perfect spot to defend the basket. At least it looked that way. At full speed, Antetokounmpo caught the pass. He leaped directly over Hardaway, who is 6 feet, 6 inches (198 cm) tall, and scored! The Bucks won the game 103-89. Antetokounmpo showed why many call him the best athlete in the NBA.

CHAPTER ONE

A STAR IS BORN

Antetokounmpo was born in Athens, Greece, on December 6, 1994. He grew up with his four brothers in Athens. As a young boy, he wasn't interested in playing basketball.

Antetokounmpo began playing basketball when he was a teenager. He tried to copy the moves of his favorite players. People around him soon began to see his basketball skills. But playing basketball wasn't Antetokounmpo's first priority. His family was poor. Even as a young child, he worked to earn money. Antetokounmpo would sell sunglasses and other items to tourists. He'd sell on the street corners in Athens. He didn't know how much his life would soon change.

⟨⟨⟨ Antetokounmpo plays near his childhood home in Athens.

THE NEXT LEVEL

Antetokounmpo quickly became an incredible basketball player. But his talent was built on a playground. He had not played enough organized basketball. Still, his height and power were impressive. He also worked very hard. When he was seventeen, he earned a chance to play with a semi-professional team in Greece.

Antetokounmpo had to walk 4 miles (6.4 kilometers) to practice every day. He wanted to make the most of his new opportunity. He dreamed of having a chance to play professional basketball. He wanted to help his family and end their financial struggles.

FACT

When he was a teenager, Antetokounmpo signed a contract to play professional basketball in Spain. The Milwaukee Bucks drafted him that same year, and he never played for the Spanish club.

>>> In 2013, Antentokounmpo played for the Greek team Filathlitikos.

CHAPTER TWO

NBA OR BUST

In 2012, Antetokounmpo played 26 games with his team. He averaged 9.5 points per game. He shot better than 62 percent from two-point range. He earned a spot in the Greek League All-Star Game. Antetokounmpo thought he might have a chance to get in the National Basketball Association (NBA.)

Teams invest millions of dollars in first-round draft picks. The goal is to get a sure thing. Many general managers want a great college player. College players compete against some of the best basketball players in the United States. Antetokounmpo didn't play college basketball. He had played one season of pro ball in Greece. Teams were afraid to draft him.

>>> Antetokounmpo celebrated with NBA commissioner
David Stern after being selected by the Milwaukee Bucks
in the 2013 NBA Draft.

On June 27, 2013, the Milwaukee Bucks decided
to take a chance. They picked Antetokounmpo. He
was the fifteenth pick in the draft. He was also the
first player drafted that season without any college
experience.

FAMILY TIES

Growing up in Athens, Antetokounmpo was poor. Today he doesn't focus on what he didn't have back then. He remembers what he did have.

"We didn't have a lot of money, but we had a lot of happiness," he said. "When we were struggling back in the day, we were all together."

Antetokounmpo played basketball with his four brothers. He dreamed of providing a better life for his family. After joining the Bucks, he got started on his dream. Antetokounmpo brought his family to America. He bought his parents a house in the same neighborhood he lived in.

FACT

When Antetokounmpo was drafted, he didn't know how to drive a car. Bucks Assistant General Manager Dave Morway gave him driving lessons.

When he was selected for his first NBA All-Star Game, Antetokounmpo was in Orlando. His mom visited to celebrate with him. His brother Thanasis called within seconds of the announcement. As always, his family was there to support him.

〉〉〉 Antetokounmpo and his family attended the 2019 NBA Awards.

CHAPTER THREE

LIFE IN THE NBA

Life in the NBA was different from playing in Greece. He was tall and fast. He had incredible skills. But in the NBA, he played every night against other big, fast players who also had great skills.

Antetokounmpo averaged 6.8 points per game as a **rookie** in his first season. It was the lowest scoring average of his career. He started 23 of the 77 games of the season.

FACT

Before a game during his rookie season, Antetokounmpo didn't have enough money with him to take a cab to the arena. He had sent all his money to his family in Greece. He had to run through the streets of Milwaukee. A fan eventually picked him up and gave him a ride to the game!

>>> Antetokounmpo protects the ball from Chicago Bulls players Derrick Rose and Jimmy Butler in 2015.

Although he had a low scoring average, Antetokounmpo showed flashes of what earned him his nickname. He pulled down 339 rebounds. He added 60 steals and 61 blocks. He proved he was a solid **two-way player**.

RISING STAR

Antetokounmpo began the 2014–15 season as a starter. He showed great improvements in every category in his second year. In 81 games, he averaged almost 13 points per game. He improved his accuracy too.

Antetokounmpo also helped the Bucks improve from their last few seasons. The Bucks had better teamwork. Antetokounmpo was one of the players on the team that had the most game time. He helped Milwaukee return to the playoffs.

Antetokounmpo made his playoff **debut** on April 15, 2015. He played against the Chicago Bulls. Three minutes into the game, he scored his first points.

About ten minutes into the game, Antetokounmpo was bringing the ball up court. The ball was knocked away from him. Antetokounmpo didn't give up. He chased the ball into the backcourt. He quickly gathered it and sped up the court. With his long strides, Antetokounmpo weaved through the Bulls defense. He glided to the basket and scored. This was just one example of Antetokounmpo's skills at play in the game.

>>> Antetokounmpo shoots in the 2015 NBA Playoffs.

The Bucks lost the series 4-2. But Antetokounmpo had earned valuable playoff experience. With his teammates, he wanted to bring a championship title to Milwaukee.

DOMINATION

The 2016–17 season was a turning point for Antetokounmpo. He had three full seasons in the NBA. He was ready to **dominate**. Offensively, he broke out. His 22.9 points per game was a career high. Offensively, players are judged on three important categories. These are points, **assists**, and rebounds. Antetokounmpo led the Bucks in all three.

Soon his dominant play was recognized nationally. At the 2017 All-Star Game, Antetokounmpo led the East team. He scored 30 points. In 2019, he was the captain of the East All-Star team. He finished the game as the leading scorer with 38 points. His hard work earned him the NBA's Most Improved Player award.

FACT

After three years of playing in the NBA, Antetokounmpo had to return to his native Greece to serve in the military. It is a law in Greece that every man serve his country, even an NBA star!

>>> Antetokounmpo dunks over Stephen Curry of the Golden
State Warriors in the 2017 NBA All-Star Game.

CHAPTER FOUR

POSTSEASON POWER

Expectations in Milwaukee were high as the 2018–19 season began. Antetokounmpo and his teammates didn't disappoint. The Bucks finished the regular season with a record of 60-22. The pressure was on Antetokounmpo. His team couldn't be knocked out in the first round.

The first round was against the Detroit Pistons. He averaged 26 points and 12 rebounds per game. The Bucks easily swept the Pistons 4-0 to advance to the semifinals. They prepared to face the strong Boston Celtics. It would be the first time Antetokounmpo played a second-round playoff game.

FACT

Antetokounmpo's older brother Thanasis is also a basketball player. In July 2019, he signed with the Bucks, joining his brother on the team.

>>> Antetokounmpo lines up a shot over the Boston Celtics'
Aron Baynes in a 2018 game.

The Bucks lost the opening game 112-90.
Then they won four games to send Boston home.
Antetokounmpo played his best in the game-four win.
He led the Bucks in points with 39. His 68 percent
field goal shooting was a career best. The Bucks were
cruising. Their star player averaged 27 points per
game during the season. Antetokounmpo and the
Bucks were close to the NBA Finals!

BACK TO THE PLAYOFFS

All eyes were on Antetokounmpo as he and his team faced off against the Toronto Raptors in the 2019 Eastern Conference Finals. In game one, the Bucks didn't start off well. The Raptors had tough defense. The Bucks couldn't get past them. Antetokounmpo still had six points scored in the first four minutes of the game. At halftime, the Raptors were ahead 59-51. The Milwaukee crowd cheered on the Bucks. The Bucks turned the game around as the Raptors started to lose steam. The Bucks won the game 108-100. Antetokounmpo scored 24 points during the game.

>>> Antetokounmpo drives against Jonas Valanciunas of the Raptors in 2017.

<<<< Antetokounmpo celebrates after scoring in a playoff game.

Playoff History

Antetokounmpo reached the playoffs with his team in four of his first six seasons. His first three playoff appearances in 2015, 2017, and 2018 ended quickly. The Bucks were eliminated in the first round. Yet Antetokounmpo still has impressive career numbers in the postseason. He averaged 23 points per game in 34 playoff games. He has also shown improvement year to year. His highest scoring game in the 2015 playoffs was 17 points.

MISSED OPPORTUNITY

It was game two of the 2019 Eastern Conference Finals against the Raptors. Antetokounmpo never slowed down. The Bucks cruised to a 125-103 win. The Bucks led the series 2-0. They had won six playoff games in a row. The Bucks seemed close to winning the NBA championship. Suddenly, it all went wrong.

〉〉〉 Antetokounmpo scores in game two of the 2019 NBA Playoffs.

In game three, Antetokounmpo went ice cold shooting. He scored just 12 points. The game was tied 103-103 in the second overtime. Antetokounmpo made a crucial mistake. He was called for a **blocking foul**. There were 4 minutes left to play. The Bucks' best player had fouled out of the game. Without him, the Raptors were able to take over. They won game three, 118-112.

The Bucks never seemed to recover from the loss. After that, Antetokounmpo and the Bucks lost four straight games. Antetokounmpo and the Bucks were going home.

MVP

Kawhi Leonard. James Harden. Kyrie Irving. Steph Curry. Kevin Durant. The NBA is full of superstars who had great seasons in 2018-19. None were considered better than Antetokounmpo. He was named the NBA's Most Valuable Player on June 24, 2019. Voters saw his dominant numbers on the court. Antetokounmpo finished the season averaging 27.7 points per game, third in the NBA. He pulled down 12.5 rebounds per game and added nearly six assists each game.

CHAPTER FIVE

RISING EXPECTATIONS

The 2018-19 season was a disappointment for Antetokounmpo. He had the best personal season of his career. He led the Bucks to the top in the Eastern Conference. They were the favorite for the NBA Finals from the East. Then they were badly outplayed by the Raptors.

Critics say Antetokounmpo doesn't have what it takes to lead a team. They point to the 2018-19 playoffs as evidence. The truth is no one player can carry a team. Antetokounmpo averaged 25.5 points per game in the playoffs. He collected more than 12 rebounds per game. The Bucks just faced a team that was on a roll.

〉〉〉 Antetokounmpo playing for Greece in the 2014 FIBA World Cup.

Going for the Gold

Antetokounmpo is proud of his Greek **heritage**.
He has represented his country in international
tournaments several times. He was a member of the
2014 Greek National team that competed for the
FIBA World Cup. The nation of Greece is hoping
Antetokounmpo will stay healthy and be part of the
country's 2020 Olympic squad.

BRIGHT FUTURE

Antetokounmpo is only 25 years old. He is entering the prime of his NBA career. He is a competitor. He wants to lead his team to the NBA title. Following the playoffs in 2019, Antetokounmpo let his fans know what his offseason plans were. He said he would "come back again next year and be a better basketball player and a better teammate." Basketball experts believe if he follows this plan, he could soon be holding the NBA championship trophy high over his head!

TIMELINE

1994 Antetokounmpo is born in Athens, Greece, on December 6

2011 Joins the Greek semi-professional team Filathlitikos

2012 Signs a four-year contract to play professional basketball with CAI Zaragoza in Spain

2012 Signs a contract to endorse Nikes that pays him $25,000 per year

2013 Declares himself for the 2013 NBA Draft

2013 Drafted 15th overall in the first round of the NBA Draft by the Milwaukee Bucks on June 27

2013 Signs his rookie contract with the Bucks on July 30

2014 Plays for Greece in the World Cup. He averages 6.3 points per game in six games.

2015 Reaches the playoffs for the first time in his career. He averages 11.5 points per game

2016 Signs a four-year, $100 million contract extension to stay in Milwaukee

2017 Named to the NBA All-Star game for the first time

2017 Wins NBA Most Improved Player Award

2019 Scores a career high 52 points in a 130-125 loss to the 76ers

GLOSSARY

ASSIST (uh-SIST)—a pass that leads to a score by a teammate

BLOCKING FOUL (blok-ing foul)— a foul called when a player gets in front of the ball handler and keeps him from moving forward

DEBUT (dey-BYOO)—the first appearance of a person or thing

DOMINATE (dom-uh-neyt)—to control and perform better than another person or team

FIELD GOAL (FEELD GOHL)—a successful shot taken from the court while the game is in play; if shot from in front of the three-point line, these are worth two points, if shot from behind the three-point line, these are worth three points

HERITAGE (her-i-tij)—something passed down to a person by birth as a tradition

ROOKIE (ruk-EE)—a player who is playing their first year on a team

SEED (SEED)—how a team is ranked based on the team's region and conference

READ MORE

Chandler, Matt. *Pro Basketball Records: A Guide for Every Fan.* North Mankato, MN: Compass Point Books, 2019.

Nagelhout, Ryan. *Talk Like a Basketball Player.* New York: Gareth Stevens Publishing, 2017.

Omoth, Tyler. *Lebron James: Basketball Superstar.* North Mankato, MN: Capstone Press, 2019.

INTERNET SITES

NBA
www.nba.com

Milwaukee Bucks
www.milwaukeebucks.com

Basketball Hall of Fame
www.hoophall.com

INDEX